CW00470580

San Diego Travel Guide

The Top 10 Highlights in San Diego

Table of Contents

Introduction to San Diego

Not only is San Diego one of the most beautiful cities in the United States, it can also compete with any other city in the world. Famous for its pristine coastlines, constant sunshine and electric nightlife, this city offers no shortage of sights and attractions. Situated in the state of California, the "City by the Bay" has something for everyone because San Diego truly has it all.

Arguably the most colorful of San Diego's attractions, Old Town dates back to the time of the arrival of the early Spaniards in California. Old Town San Diego has been designed to reflect the history of early California via daily shows, monthly festivities, artisan works, dining opportunities and a host of beautiful stores that give the area a festive air that you shouldn't miss out on.

Meanwhile, visitors to San Diego's Gaslamp Quarter can expect to be dazzled by 21 blocks of sidewalk cafes, open air restaurants, microbreweries, resident artists, jazz clubs and late night dancing. Regarded as the historic heart of San Diego, the Gaslamp Quarter is worth a visit while in San Diego.

Lined with picturesque buildings, flowing fountains, plush lawns and over 25 museums, Balboa Park is regarded as the largest urban cultural park in the United States. The park is also home to theaters, carousels, shops and many more attractions worth a visit. Spend a day at Balboa Park, the definitive cultural hub of San Diego, and soak up the stunning setting as you explore the attractions it houses.

While it may be tempting to spend your entire vacation exploring, don't forget to leave some time for a history lesson in America's finest city. Head over to the Maritime Museum of San Diego, a well regarded and highly interactive museum that shows off the maritime heritage of the city.

Your trip to San Diego will not be complete without spending some time at one of its numerous picturesque beaches. While the immaculate beaches to enjoy are many, the absolute must-see stretch of beach is found at Coronado Silver Strand.

Beach lovers will also delight at the wonderful natural offerings of Shell Beach in La Jolla; although there's much more to La Jolla than its spectacular beaches. Go here to admire the beautiful town that's ringed with blue waters, and which just happens to be one of the prettiest Oceanside towns in California.

San Diego's coastal seat makes for an ideal destination for the adventurous at heart. Whether you are hiking along sandstone cliffs, or strolling through the frothy surf of dazzling beaches, you'll find little reason to stray far from the natural wonders of this amazing American city. San

Diego's numerous and varied activities are designed to ensure that you don't have the time to get bored during your visit.

1. Balboa Park

Situated in El Prado, Balboa Park is the largest cultural complex west of the Mississippi. Boasting a high concentration of cultural institutions within its boundaries, Balboa Park was originally built in 1915. Full of architectural grandeur, cultural treasures, stunning gardens, lush landscapes and award-winning performing arts, it will take you more than a day to see it all.

While the buildings at Balboa Park are beautiful enough to be regarded as attractions in themselves, the real draw here is the culture, science, history and arts that are enclosed within their walls. Among the attractions found in this magnificent cultural complex are 15 museums, 8 major gardens, a botanical building, outdoor gardens and a Tony Award-winning theater.

Balboa Park's many museums cover every interest, from the Museum of Man to the Museum of Art. With over 15 museums, the park is one of the richest cultural areas in the western United States.

Highlights of the Balboa Park major gardens included the Botanical Building. This was the largest wood lath structure in the world when it was built in 1915. Today it is home to 2,100 permanent specimens of tropical plants. Also visit the Japanese Friendship Garden, and the Zoro Garden which is a sunken butterfly garden.

Palm Canyon is an oasis that contains 450 palms. The Inez Grant Parker Memorial Rose Garden was voted as one of the world's top rose gardens. Desert Garden features 2.5 acres of drought-resistant plants and succulents from all around the world.

Visitors can also enjoy performance arts at Balboa Park. The Old Globe Theatre was the winner of the 1984 Tony Award for Outstanding Regional Theatre, and currently produces 14 works on 3 stages annually. Also visit the Marie Hitchcock Puppet Theatre where you will find performers with lots of strings attached.

At the Starlight Bowl, you can enjoy performances by the Starlight Musical Theater during July and August. Also worth a peek is the Spreckels Organ Pavilion, one of the largest outdoor pipe organs in the world. It hosts year-round Sunday organ concerts, in addition to the annual Summer International Organ Festival.

If you plan on visiting more than two of the numerous attractions found here, consider getting the Balboa Park Passport which is available at any of the 13 attractions it can get you into. For an even better deal, plan your visit on the days that offer free admission into 2-5 locations each week.

2. Old Town

Most visitors to Old Town San Diego go for shopping at the numerous stores that stock nice handicrafts. Others go to enjoy a large platter of enchiladas and tacos, washed down with a margarita. But history buffs can also get their fix by poking around inside the historic buildings of Old Town, as they imagine life in early California.

As the first European settlement in what is now California, Old Town San Diego's roots were founded when a Spanish mission was built there in 1769. But by the 1820s, the settlers had moved into Gaslamp Quarter, closer to the water, leaving their "old town" behind.

Nestled in the heart of San Diego, Old Town San Diego is centered on the oldest area of the first European settlement, and includes a state historic park and related historic sites situated outside the park.

The State Historic Park takes up 9 square blocks and preserves numerous historic structures, five of which were built of adobe bricks. These include the first schoolhouse in California, the first newspaper office in the state, a stable and a blacksmith shop.

The preserved buildings are each a small museum in themselves which provide a glimpse into San Diego life between the years 1821 and 1872. The historic buildings offer a good way of learning about the early history of California.

Old Town is where you get to learn about life during the Mexican and early American periods, as the cultures converged to transform San Diego from a Mexican pueblo into a European settlement. The historic plaza is a gathering ground for community events, fiesta, historical activities, living history programs, as well as numerous restaurants, museums and retail shops that surround the plaza.

A pleasant cultural experience awaits every visitor to Old Town San Diego, the birthplace of California. Here you can get a glimpse into early California through the 20 museums, art galleries, artisans and shops.

Visitors can also enjoy live entertainment from folkloric dancers, mariachis and artists. Fine or casual dining opportunities abound in the multiple regional and international cuisines available at this site that has the highest concentration of Mexican restaurants in the entire San Diego area.

Old Town offers a romantic and charming mix of whitewashed mud brick buildings with Spanish tile roofs; while the wooden storefronts resemble something straight out of an Old West town.

The shops found here today mostly sell Mexican-style pottery, tinwork and more. Go on a pleasant stroll here, while window shopping. You can also extend your route to outside the park and head down San Diego Avenue.

Another fun way of connecting with California's past is via the Living History demonstrations of life during the 19th century. Fans of the paranormal can join in the Old Town ghost tours that begin from in front of Casa de Reyes during the evenings.

The park also hosts many celebrations of holidays and historic events. In December, visitors can attend Holiday in the Park, which features performance tours and recreations of the holidays in the 1860s. In addition to the specialty festivals which are held year-round at Old Town, the largest celebrations of *Dia de los Muertos* and *Cinco de Mayo* in the city of San Diego take place here.

At the edge of the State Historic Park is the Old Town Market which offers more shopping opportunities. Here you can enjoy a tour of a reconstructed 1853 adobe house, a restored convent dating from 1908, and a new theatre. There is also a museum full of archaeological finds. Another Old Town historic site in the area but situated outside the confines of the state park include the "haunted" Whaley House.

3. Gaslamp Quarter

With origins dating from the mid-19th century, Gaslamp Quarter is situated in downtown San Diego, near the Convention Center.

The attraction rises from blocks of Victorian-era buildings and modern skyscrapers that stand side by side, and houses over 100 of the finest restaurants, nightclubs, pubs and retail shops in San Diego. The District is a veritable playground rich in cultural offering that includes art galleries, concert venues, symphony halls, museums and theaters.

An area of great architectural charm, the Gaslamp Quarter has streets lined with original nineteenth-century buildings, along with others moved in from different parts of San Diego, all restored to their original exuberance. Restaurants, clubs and shops now occupy the former salons and brothels. Walk the streets and admire the historic buildings.

A random walk in Gaslamp Quarter will give you a sense of the place, allowing you to enjoy pleasant buildings, do some shopping, and enjoy a bite to eat. Visit the restaurants, night clubs and shops. Boutique shops offer interesting wares alongside souvenir vendors, with Horton Plaza comprising the local shopping center.

Visitors can easily spend an entire day in Gaslamp Quarter, shopping at one of the numerous retail stores at Horton Plaza. Lovers of the paranormal will enjoy the night-time ghost tour of the Gaslamp Quarter, which makes for a good alternative for those who wish to be out at night but don't want to go clubbing. Also visit some of the museums and be thrilled by their interactive exhibits.

Dining options also abound with plenty of opportunities for al fresco dining on the sidewalks of this cosmopolitan and dynamic district. You can have your meal sky high on a rooftop lounge, or inside an intimate restaurant featuring ornate designs.

On a cool California evening, the Gaslamp Quarter transforms into a sophisticated playground under a sparkling night sky. This is when thousands of residents and tourists come out in style for a night of fine dining, live theater, craft cocktails, music and dancing. Enjoy a signature cocktail made by a creative mixologist at a rooftop bar or groove the night away at a happening night club.

There's nothing like sipping a cold drink at an outdoor patio on a warm day. And you can do this from one of Gaslamp Quarter's rooftop bars as you enjoy panoramic views of the downtown, Coronado Bridge and San Diego Bay.

4. Coronado Beach

There's a quiet, laid-back simplicity to Coronado that visitors enjoy, in addition to its beautiful views of the downtown San Diego skyline. But it's the white sandy beaches of Coronado that have consistently earned it many ratings as one of the top ten beaches in America.

Situated on the Coronado peninsula just across the Big Bay, across the bay from downtown San Diego, Coronado Beach is a great beach for every type of beach lover. With Downtown Coronado nearby, the beach offers gentle waves and lots of fine, clean sand. Its surroundings are also pretty with the interesting architecture of Hotel Del Coronado displayed beautifully on the oceanfront.

Coronado Beach is a lovely place to take a stroll. Take off your shoes and walk barefoot at the surf's edge, or stay on the paved pathway close by, stopping to watch the sun set from one of the benches. To avoid the crowds, head over to north Coronado Beach which is less busy. The beach is ideal for simply roaming around and playing in the sand. You can also attend the fun evening bonfire on the beach.

The most popular section of Coronado Beach is situated around the Hotel Del Coronado. This must-see hotel is said to be the inspiration behind Emerald City in *The Wizard of Oz*. The sprawling rusty red and white, Victorian-style seaside hotel was opened in 1888. Today a national historic landmark, the hotel has hosted many famous and infamous of the 20th century, and is also said to house a resident ghost!

The legendary hotel is an American treasure with more than 125 years of stories to tell. It is said that the founders of the hotel dreamed of creating a seaside resort that would be "the talk of the Western world" – and they did. Since then, the resort has become a living legend visited by dignitaries, celebrities and presidents.

Rated by USA Today as one of the top 10 hotels in the world, the Del Coronado continues to maintain its rich history while offering contemporary conveniences such as unique beachfront dining experiences, shopping, an award-winning spa, and various recreational activities. The spectacular setting of the hotel, its award-winning service and impeccable cuisine also deserve mention.

Consistently named one of the best in the world, the hotel features a number of amazing ocean view bars and restaurants and breathtaking Victorian architecture with its signature red turrets. You don't have to stay at the hotel to enjoy it. Visitors can browse the historic photographs and exhibits or enjoy a nice meal on the terrace.

The Coronado Peninsula is also famous for the distinctive San Diego-Coronado Bridge that is worth a peek during your visit here.

But beyond its architectural marvels, Coronado's island community offers visitors an experience that is worlds apart, with a charming quaintness typical of small towns, old-world mansions, elegant gardens, unique shopping experiences and dining options with spectacular ocean views. It's no wonder that the region has been dubbed "The Crown City" after Coronado which is Spanish for "the crowned one".

5. Maritime Museum of San Diego

Situated along the San Diego waterfront on Harbor Drive, beneath sleek downtown high-rise buildings is the Maritime Museum of San Diego. The history of San Diego is tied to the sea, and the collection of the Maritime Museum features vessels that illustrate seaport activities from the world over. The Maritime Museum appeals to visitors of every type.

Whether your interest is to learn more about maritime history or you just have a thing for really cool ships, you are certain to enjoy exploring the Maritime Museum of San Diego. What makes this museum particularly appealing and special is the fact that it has 5 different ships that you can go onto and explore. These ships range from an old-fashioned yacht, a 19th century exploration ship and submarines.

The Maritime Museum of San Diego does not even give off the typical museum-in-a-building feel, seeing as it is spread out along the San Diego harbor, inside various ships.

The museum is housed in one of the world's finest collections of historic ships, with the majestic and iconic Star of India docked in downtown San Diego on the beautiful waterfront.

The Star of India is the oldest active sailing ship in the world. During her lengthy maritime career, this sturdy iron ship hauled freight to India from England, and also carried immigrants to New Zealand from England. It also packed salmon in the Bering Sea. The Star of India was fully restored in 1976 and is today maintained to illustrate her role as an immigrant ship.

During your tour of the Star of India, you will be shocked by the 20th century living quarters that the immigrants who were sailing to a new life from England to New Zealand had to contend with.

There are many ships to see at the museum, although some stand out in the minds of visitors as their favorites. Other ships you can admire at the Maritime Museum include The Berkeley, The Californian and the submarines.

The Berkeley is an 1898 Victorian-style steam ferryboat that carried passengers on the San Francisco Bay between 1898 and 1973. This elegant, 19th century landmark has the wooden benches in the restored main passenger decks illuminated through stained glass windows. The lower deck houses displays and a model ship-building workshop.

The opulent Medea steam yacht is just the ship to board and explore for those who may be curious as to how the wealthy sailed around during the early 1900s.

Visitors to the Maritime Museum can also squeeze and wriggle their way through submarines such as the Soviet-era B-39 and the American USS Dolphin. The B-39 is a diesel-electric submarine that was commissioned during the early 1970s by the Soviet Navy, and which served for over 20 years on active duty.

With this tour, you will quickly learn just how cramped life underwater can be, as you navigate the narrow hallways and climb through circular holes to get from one room to the next. You will also encounter a working periscope that is very neat to look through.

The Californian is the official tall ship of the State of California which was built in 1984. The ship is a replica of an 1847 vessel that brought law and order to the coast of California during the Gold Rush. The Pilot is a ship that was used to transfer harbor pilots to incoming ships. The boat had the longest career of any working boat in the Western hemisphere, which spanned the years 1914 to 1996.

The museum encourages hands on experiences. Visitors can go sailing, whale watching or simply cruise around the bay on many of the museum's ships. The museum also houses a world renowned research library and a retail shop with many souvenirs for sale, as well as academic and historic books.

Some of the exhibits hosted at the museum include the Age of Steam, the Age of Sail, San Diego's Navy, Harvesting the Ocean and Charting the Sea. There are also rotating and seasonal exhibits as well. During your tour, you will learn how the ships were used in the past for exploration and for battle.

The Maritime Museum of San Diego hosts a range of special events on a regular basis such as the Festival of Sail which is held every 3 years. During this event, a tall ship armada joins the historic vessels at the Maritime Museum, as the waterfront comes alive with mock cannon battle cruises, tall ship parades and plenty of dockside entertainment.

6. La Jolla

Situated a 20-minute drive north of downtown San Diego, "La Jolla" is Spanish for "the jewel", a fitting name for an attractive town ringed with beautiful blue waters. La Jolla is one of the prettiest Oceanside towns in California, and home to several of the best beaches in the state.

When people say San Diego has great beaches, what they really mean is that La Jolla has great beaches. La Jolla Shores, La Jolla Cave and Windansea are not only the best in San Diego but perhaps even the best in the entire state.

In fact, La Jolla Shores may be the most beautiful in California with its wide, gently sloping beach and panoramic views. A sunset or morning walk here is enough to relax even the most stressed out. Your walk will be even better when the tide is going out, leaving a mirror-like water layer to coat the sand.

Take the steps that go down next to 1298 Prospect where you can enjoy a private walk with places to sit and enjoy the view. Follow the wooden fence behind the entrance to the cave, and then walk along the dirt path. You will find a few people here, but you will not be alone as a large colony of cormorants and seagulls inhabit the cliff face below.

If you are planning the perfect southern California vacation, look no further than La Jolla. This popular San Diego destination offers plenty of activities for visitors including cultural institutions, outdoor activities and more. There's something for everyone who goes to explore this beach town.

La Jolla offers a broad spectrum of activities from casual fine dining, to museums, art galleries and one-of-a-kind boutiques, not to mention the slew of fun outdoor activities.

Go on a self-guided tour and visit the art galleries, the Sunny Jim sea cave, the La Jolla waterfront and the hidden mermaid statue. Take a stroll and do some window-shopping in boutiques that line Prospect Avenue and the side streets running into it. If you enjoy the theatre, the La Jolla Playhouse is worth a visit.

Popular with outdoor adventurers who go to kayak, dive or surf here, La Jolla also boasts well-groomed hiking trails that offer spectacular views. Go hiking through the trails of Torrey Pines. Bring a picnic lunch to Scripps Park which lies along the dramatic coastline. Here you can also enjoy concerts under the stars.

La Jolla is also a top foodie destination, with some of the best-rated restaurants in San Diego. The town is home to a number of top-notch restaurants, many of which serve excellent cuisines. Go here to enjoy fine dining opportunities with spectacular ocean views.

La Jolla also hosts a series of annual events you should know about. The La Jolla Festival of the Arts is one of

California's top rated art festivals, which is held in late June. Also attend the La Jolla Concerts by the Sea for free concerts which are held every Sunday from June through August.

That said the biggest draw for tourists and locals alike in La Jolla are its beaches. Go here to swim, snorkel, scuba dive and surf. Also explore the tide pools and coves along La Jolla Shores. All in all, La Jolla is simply a great place to just go and relax. With its dramatic coastline that boasts spectacular views, it's no wonder that La Jolla is one of California's most popular beach destinations.

Surrounded on 3 sides by the sea, and backed by Mount Soledad's steep slopes, the coastal profile and quaint village lifestyle of La Jolla evokes a Mediterranean feel. With a unique microclimate coupled with unmatched natural beauty, the casual vibe and world-class attractions, La Jolla certainly lives up to its nickname as San Diego's "jewel by the sea".

7. Carlsbad Flower Fields

Each year, southern California ushers in the spring season with a very special attraction – the Flower Fields at Carlsbad Ranch. One of southern California's most unique attractions, and an annual rite of ushering in spring, the Flower Fields feature a dazzling rainbow of splendid Ranunculus flowers set on a hillside overlooking the striking coastline.

The Carlsbad Flower Fields are quite a sight for sore eyes if you're driving north of San Diego, as you are dazzled by hillsides awash in brilliant colors. The Flower Fields are a throwback to a different era in the region of San Diego. The working flower farm comprises a 50-acre swath of blossoms, covered in yellow, purple, orange, green and red. The Flower Fields are located in Carlsbad, north of downtown San Diego.

While the fields may look like a botanical garden - they are not. This is the location of a grower of Giant Ranunculus bulbs. Because the flowers these bulbs produce are so beautiful, people go to admire them. This creates a temporary tourist attraction at every spring.

The Carlsbad Flower Fields main attraction is the pretty Giant Ranunculus flowers, with their vibrant colors and dense petals. The Ranunculus flowers come into full bloom in March and April, when they unveil their rose-like petals.

The flowers splash the hillsides in a rainbow of colors. It is during these two and a half months of spring that the fields are open to the public.

In addition to the beautiful show of blossoms in the Fields, there is a Miniature Rose Garden, a maze of sweet pea and poinsettia greenhouse, as well as a display that features each of the 180-plus All-American Rose selection winners since 1940.

In addition to the vivid color bands, visitors can also enjoy rides on tractor driven wagons, or stroll through a massive greenhouse filled with the world famous Ecke poinsettias. You can also navigate the pathways of a sweet pea maze and enjoy the numerous varieties of themed gardens.

Take a leisurely stroll along the field pathways that offers you the opportunity of experiencing colorful bands of the Ranunculus flowers up close, as well as enjoy breathtaking views of the Pacific Ocean. A walk through the dirt fields on the hillside overlooking the Pacific Ocean in the distance makes for a very pleasant experience. Be sure to bring your camera to take wonderful pictures of the colorful blooms.

Go here to take in the beauty of flowers. The Flower Fields make for a great spot to go for a day out, have a picnic and enjoy the beautiful weather of southern California. Picnic tables are available for the convenience of visitors. Throughout the season, the Flower Fields also host a series of Special Events which are designed to entertain visitors of every type.

The flowers are also available for sale as stems. Visitors can also purchase Flower Fields brand products at its store which is located on site.

8. Museum of Contemporary Art

Situated on Kettner Boulevard, the Museum of Contemporary Art San Diego provides access to the best of western art of our time within two great locations: at La Jolla and in Downtown San Diego.

The downtown site captures the vibrancy and energy of the city, with its site-specific installations, and soaring exhibition spaces that formerly housed the baggage building of the Santa Fe Depot.

The museum offers a unique variety of experiences for the San Diego community, by showcasing a collection that is internally recognized, in addition to hosting an ever-changing schedule of public programs and exhibitions.

One of the highlights of the museum is San Diego's most creatively lit stairwell with installations. Visitors to the museum can also enjoy an evening of art, music and cocktails on Thursday nights.

The Museum's location in La Jolla is in Prospect Street and one of the highlights to watch out for is the outdoor Sculpture Garden. Visitors can also browse the museum's X-Store which features one-of-a-kind gifts including books, jewelry, home décor and more.

Whether you opt to visit the Museum of Contemporary Art's location in Downtown San Diego or at La Jolla, you will find the same things: world-class art in rotating exhibitions and interesting public programs. You will also fine works from the permanent collection of the museum by promising and emerging talent, as well as major figures of the international contemporary art scene.

9. San Diego Air & Space Museum

Situated in Pan American Plaza, the San Diego Air & Space Museum is the setting in which science, space and the history of aviation unfold.

The museum is California's official air and space museum which holds a collection of historic spacecraft and aircraft from all across the globe, including the actual Apollo 9 Command Module spacecraft; a flyable replica of Lindbergh's Spirit of St. Louis; and the world's only real GPS satellite on display.

It is noteworthy that the Apollo 9 Command Module was actually flown in space, while thee replica of the Spirit of St. Louis was built by some of its original designers.

The San Diego Air & Space Museum features interactive exhibits such as MaxFlight simulators in addition to dynamic and hands-on temporary exhibitions. The museum also hosts Balboa Park's first 3D/4D Theater and the Flight Path Grill of the Alaska Airlines.

The museum has also featured a special exhibit to commemorate the 70 anniversary of the ending of the Second World War. The exhibit showcases a rare collection of items from the war's early days from both the Pacific and European theaters, through the conflict's end to the rebuilding that ensued around the world following the end of the war.

The museum also boasts the second biggest aviation library and archive in the United States. Also worth a visit is the Pavilion of Flight, which is the venue for most of the San Diego Air & Space Museum's events.

10. Heritage Park

A world away from the rustic atmosphere of Old Town San Diego, Heritage Park is a Victorian village situated on a hillside, just off Juan Street. The unique and scenic Heritage Park takes visitors back to an era of a primmer San Diego and is dedicated to preserving the Victorian architecture of the city.

Following the end of the Second World War, downtown San Diego experienced a series of expansions that threatened its historic structures with demolition if they remained on their original sites. However, public and private funds paid to acquire, relocate and restore the buildings at the location that is now Heritage Park.

The Heritage Park village comprises 7 structures of classic Victorian architecture restored to their original glory on a grassy green and peaceful setting. This picturesque slice of San Diego is well worth discovery if you are in the mood to take a quiet stroll back in time.

Two buildings worth seeing in particular at Heritage Park are the Sherman-Gilbert House and the McConaughy House.

The Sherman-Gilbert House was built in 1887 and was the setting of receptions for internationally famous entertainers by the Gilbert sisters who were patrons of art and music. Artur Rubinstein played piano here, while Anna Pavlova danced in the music room.

Similarly built in 1887, the McConaughy House features the Old Town Gift Emporium held every Thursday to Tuesday, which specializes in Victorian porcelain dolls.

42845217R00022

Made in the USA
San Bernardino, CA
10 December 2016